HBJ TREASURY OF LITERATURE

A FRIEND LIKE YOU

SENIOR AUTHORS
ROGER C. FARR
DOROTHY S. STRICKLAND

AUTHORS
RICHARD F. ABRAHAMSON
ELLEN BOOTH CHURCH
BARBARA BOWEN COULTER
MARGARET A. GALLEGO
JUDITH L. IRVIN
KAREN KUTIPER
JUNKO YOKOTA LEWIS
DONNA M. OGLE
TIMOTHY SHANAHAN
PATRICIA SMITH

SENIOR CONSULTANTS
BERNICE E. CULLINAN
W. DORSEY HAMMOND
ASA G. HILLIARD III

CONSULTANTS
ALONZO A. CRIM
ROLANDO R. HINOJOSA-SMITH
LEE BENNETT HOPKINS
ROBERT J. STERNBERG

 HARCOURT BRACE JOVANOVICH, INC.
Orlando Austin San Diego Chicago Dallas New York

Printed in the United States of America

ISBN 0-15-301358-3

2 3 4 5 6 7 8 9 10   048   96   95   94   93

Acknowledgments

For permission to reprint copyrighted material, grateful acknowledgment is made to the following sources:

Barron's Educational Series, Inc.: Cover illustration from *It's Mine!* by Rod Campbell. © 1987 by Rod Campbell. Originally published by Campbell Blackie Books, London, England, 1987.

Curtis Brown, Ltd.: "Counting" from *Side By Side: Poems To Read Together* by Lee Bennett Hopkins. Text copyright © 1987 by Lee Bennett Hopkins. Published by Simon & Schuster. "I Eat My Gumdrops" from *I Was Thinking* by Freya Littledale. Text copyright © 1979 by Freya Littledale. Published by Greenwillow Books.

Child's Play (International) Ltd.: *Quick as a Cricket* by Audrey Wood, illustrated by Don Wood. © 1982 by M. Twinn.

Chronicle Books: My Friends by Taro Gomi. Copyright © 1989 by Taro Gomi; English text copyright © 1990 by Chronicle Books. Originally published in Japan by Ehonkan Publishers, Tokyo.

Lois Lenski Covey Foundation Inc.: From "All the People on Our Street" in *City Poems* by Lois Lenski. Text copyright © 1971 by Lois Lenski.

Delacorte Press, a division of Bantam Doubleday Dell Publishing Group, Inc.: Cover illustration from *Hold Tight, Bear!* by Ron Maris. Copyright © 1988 by Ron Maris. Originally published in Great Britain by Julia MacRae Books, a division of Walker Books, Ltd.

Dutton Children's Books, a division of Penguin Books USA Inc.: "Jump or Jiggle" by Evelyn Beyer from *Another Here and Now Story Book* by Lucy Sprague Mitchell. Text copyright 1937 by E. P. Dutton, renewed © 1965 by Lucy Sprague Mitchell.

Greenwillow Books, a division of William Morrow & Company, Inc.: Cover illustration from *Flying* by Donald Crews. Copyright © 1986 by Donald Crews.

Harcourt Brace Jovanovich, Inc.: I Went Walking by Sue Williams, illustrated by Julie Vivas. Text copyright © 1989 by Sue Williams; illustrations copyright © 1989 by Julie Vivas. *Silly Sally* by Audrey Wood. Copyright © 1992 by Audrey Wood.

HarperCollins Publishers: "Honey, I Love" from *Honey, I Love and Other Poems* by Eloise Greenfield, illustrated by Diane and Leo Dillon. Text copyright © 1978 by Eloise Greenfield; illustrations copyright © 1978 by Diane and Leo Dillon.

Alfred A. Knopf, Inc.: Cover illustration from *Things I Like* by Anthony Browne. Copyright © 1989 by Anthony Browne.

MGA, Inc.: Lyrics from "Willoughby, Wallaby, Woo," based on "Alligator Pie" by Dennis Lee. Lyrics copyright © by Dennis Lee.

Viking Penguin, a division of Penguin Books USA Inc.: Cover illustration from *I Like Me!* by Nancy Carlson. Copyright © 1988 by Nancy Carlson.

Handwriting models in this program have been used with permission of the publisher, Zaner-Bloser, Inc., Columbus, OH.

Photograph Credits

6–7(all), HBJ Photo; 10, HBJ Photo; 76–77(all), HBJ Photo; 81, HBJ Photo; 114–115, HBJ Photo.

Illustration Credits

Table of Contents Art
Gerald Bustamonte, left, 4; Gerald McDermott, center, 4, 5; Roseanne Litzinger, right, 5.

Unit Opening Patterns
Tracy Sabin

Bookshelf Art
Sue Williams, 6, 7

Theme Opening Art
Sue Williams, 8, 9; Rhonda Voo, 78, 79

Selection Art
Don Wood, 10–40; Diane and Leo Dillon, 41; Taro Gomi, 42–72; Tuko Fujisaki, 73; Jennie Oppenheimer, 74–75; Audrey Wood, 80–110; Chris Lewis, 111; Julie Durrell, 112–113; Julie Vivas, 114–144.

Dear Reader,

Everywhere you go you meet new people. You meet people at a party. You make new friends on a playground. Some of the friends you meet are from around the corner. Some are from around the world. Did you ever think you could meet new friends in a book?

In A Friend Like You, we have a lot of people waiting for you to meet. Turn the page and let's begin.

Sincerely,
The Authors

CONTENTS

FLYING

WRITTEN AND ILLUSTRATED BY DONALD CREWS

Climb aboard and get ready to fly through the sky in an airplane. There are many exciting things to see when you are flying high in the air.

NEW YORK TIMES BEST ILLUSTRATED

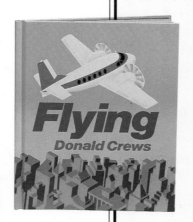

HOLD TIGHT, BEAR!

BY RON MARIS

"Bear and Raggety, Little Doll and Donkey, are going for a picnic." You can go along with them. Find out what happens to Bear when his friends fall asleep. How will Bear's friends help him?

HBJ LIBRARY BOOKS

6

I LIKE ME!
BY NANCY CARLSON

"I have a best friend. That best friend is me," says the pig in this story. Meet a happy pig who likes to have fun. She likes to draw, read, and ride fast on her bike. This pig always tries her very best. CHILDREN'S CHOICE

THINGS I LIKE
BY ANTHONY BROWNE

Did you ever meet a monkey that could paint? Painting is one of many things the young monkey in this story likes to do. AWARD-WINNING AUTHOR

IT'S MINE!
BY ROD CAMPBELL

This story takes you on a walk through some tall grass by a river. Watch out! You never know who or what you might meet along the way.

8

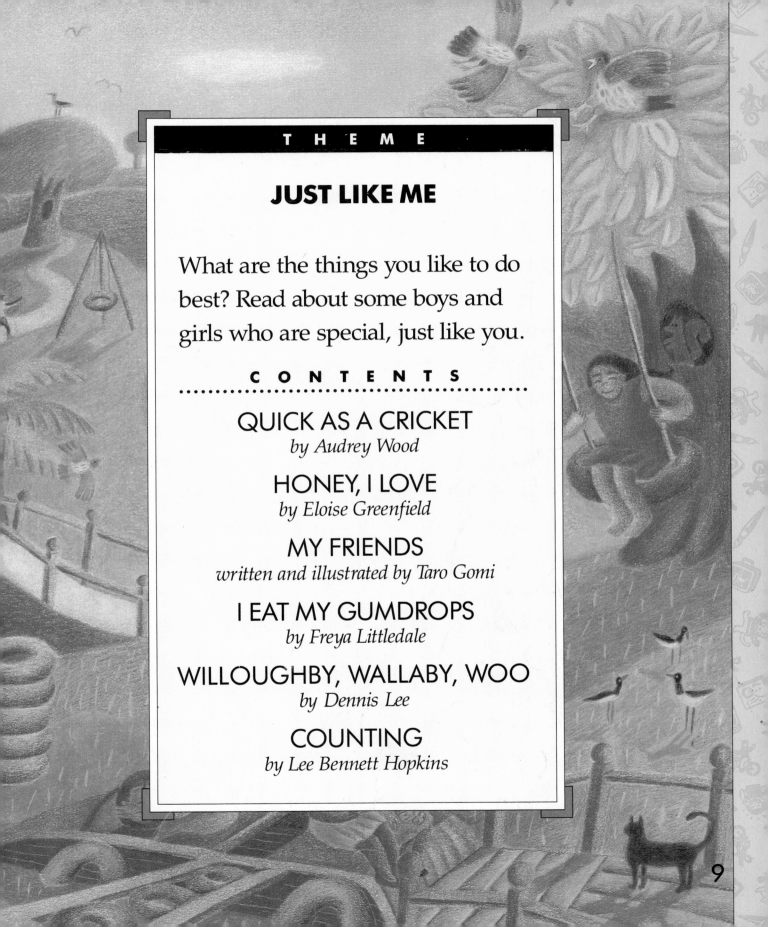

JUST LIKE ME

What are the things you like to do best? Read about some boys and girls who are special, just like you.

C O N T E N T S

I'm as quick as a cricket,

I'm as slow as a snail,

I'm as small as an ant,

I'm as large as a whale.

I'm as sad as a basset,

I'm as happy as a lark,

I'm as nice as a bunny,

I'm as mean as a shark.

I'm as cold as a toad,

I'm as hot as a fox,

I'm as weak as a kitten,

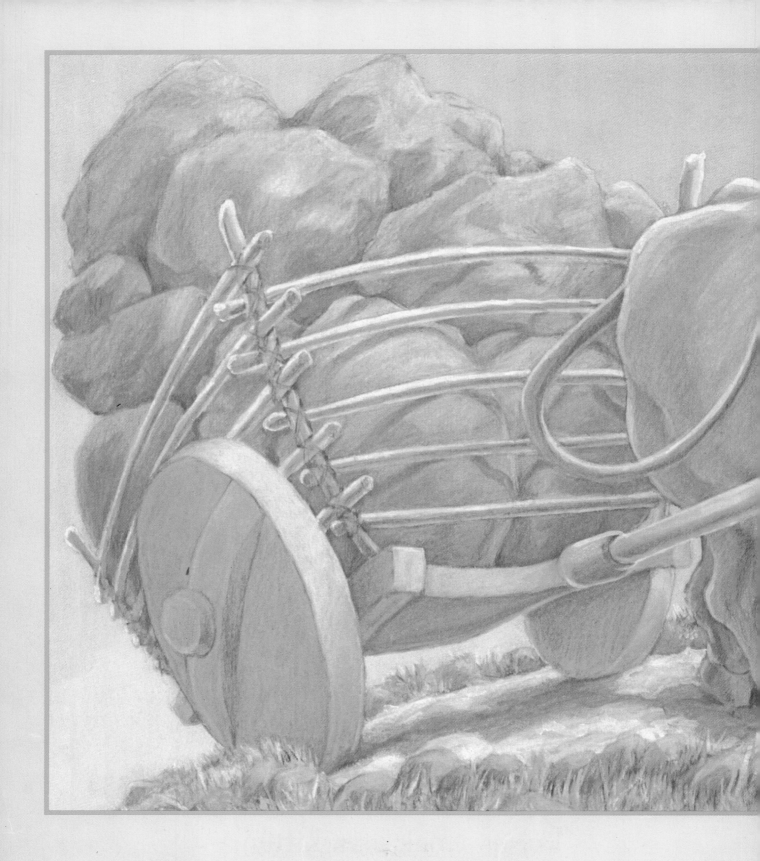

I'm as strong as an ox.

I'm as loud as a lion,

I'm as quiet as a clam,

I'm as tough as a rhino,

I'm as gentle as a lamb.

I'm as brave as a tiger,

I'm as shy as a shrimp,

I'm as tame as a poodle,

I'm as wild as a chimp.

I'm as lazy as a lizard,

I'm as busy as a bee,

Put it all together,

And you've got ME!

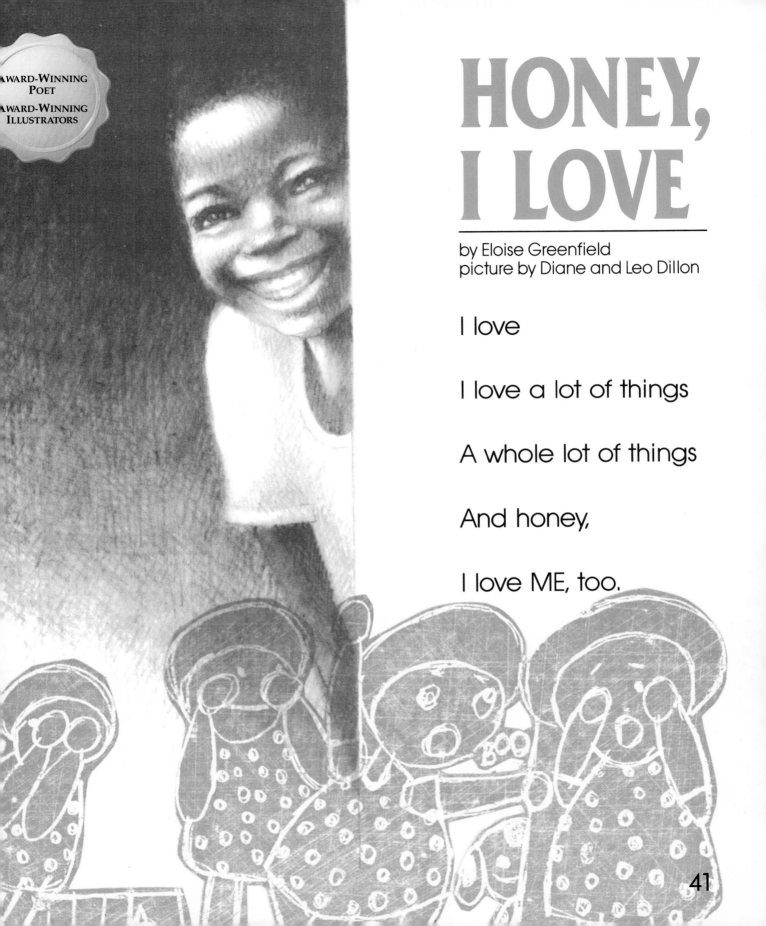

HONEY, I LOVE

by Eloise Greenfield
picture by Diane and Leo Dillon

I love

I love a lot of things

A whole lot of things

And honey,

I love ME, too.

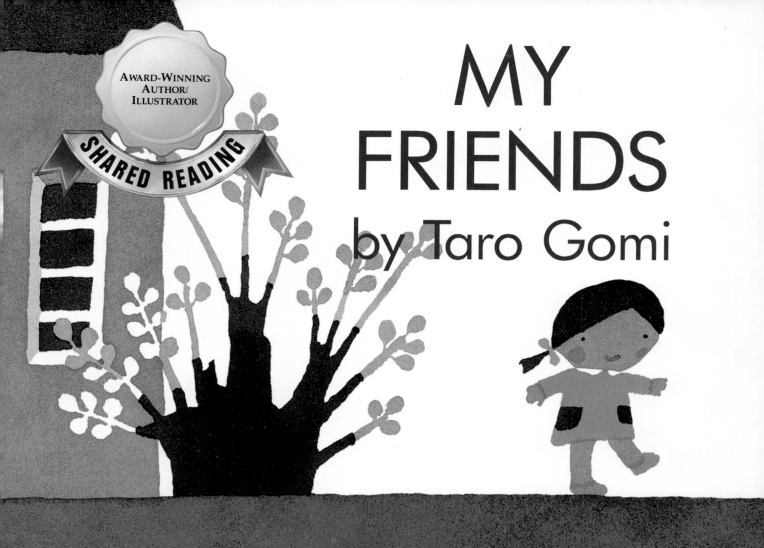

MY FRIENDS
by Taro Gomi

I learned to walk from my friend
the cat.

I learned to jump from my friend
the dog.

I learned to climb from my friend
the monkey.

I learned to run from my friend
the horse.

I learned to march from my friend the rooster.

I learned to nap from

my friend the crocodile.

I learned to smell the flowers
from my friend the butterfly.

I learned to hide from

my friend the rabbit.

I learned to explore the earth from

my friend the ant.

I learned to kick from my friend the gorilla.

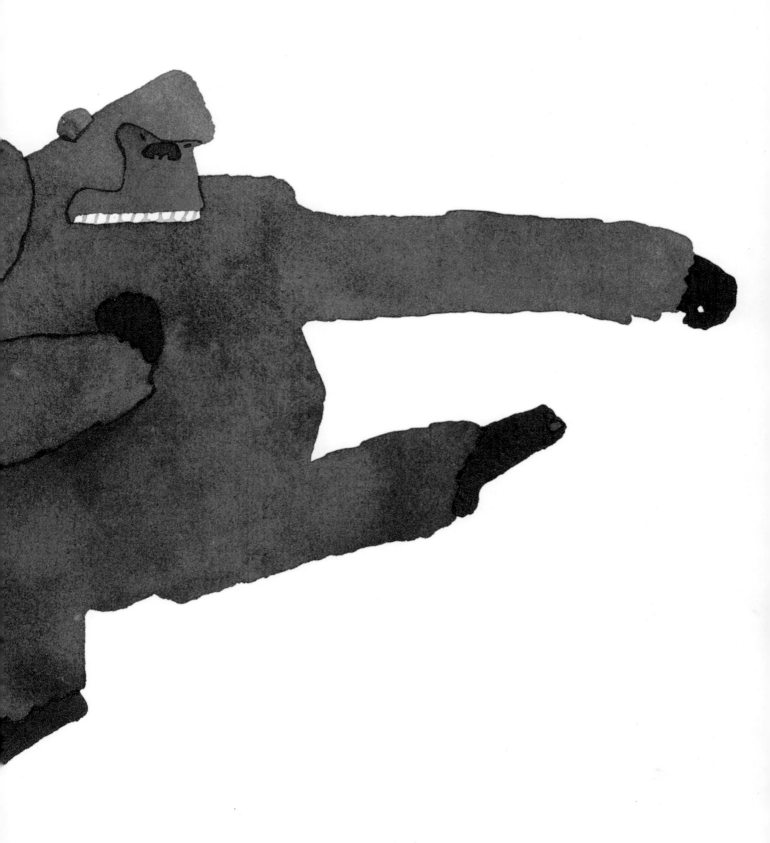

61

I learned to watch the night sky
from my friend the owl.

I learned to sing from my friends
the birds.

I learned to read from

my friends the books.

I learned to study from

my friends the teachers.

70

my friends at school.

And I learned to love from
a friend like you.

I EAT MY GUMDROPS

I eat my gumdrops
one at a time.
Red, yellow,
orange, purple—
I have a rainbow
inside me.

by Freya Littledale
illustrated by Tuko Fujisaki

73

Willoughby, Wallaby, Woo

by Dennis Lee
illustrated by Jennie Oppenheimer

Willoughby, Wallaby, Woo,
An elephant sat on you!
Willoughby Wallaby Wee,
An elephant sat on me.

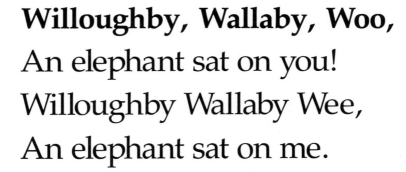

Willoughby, Wallaby, Wob,
An elephant sat on Bob.
Willoughby Wallaby Wommy,
An elephant sat on Tommy.

Counting

Lee Bennett Hopkins

AWARD-WINNING AUTHOR

1-2
I love you.

3-4
I love you more.

5-6
Fiddlesticks!

7-8
I think you're great.

9-10
Let's start counting all over again.

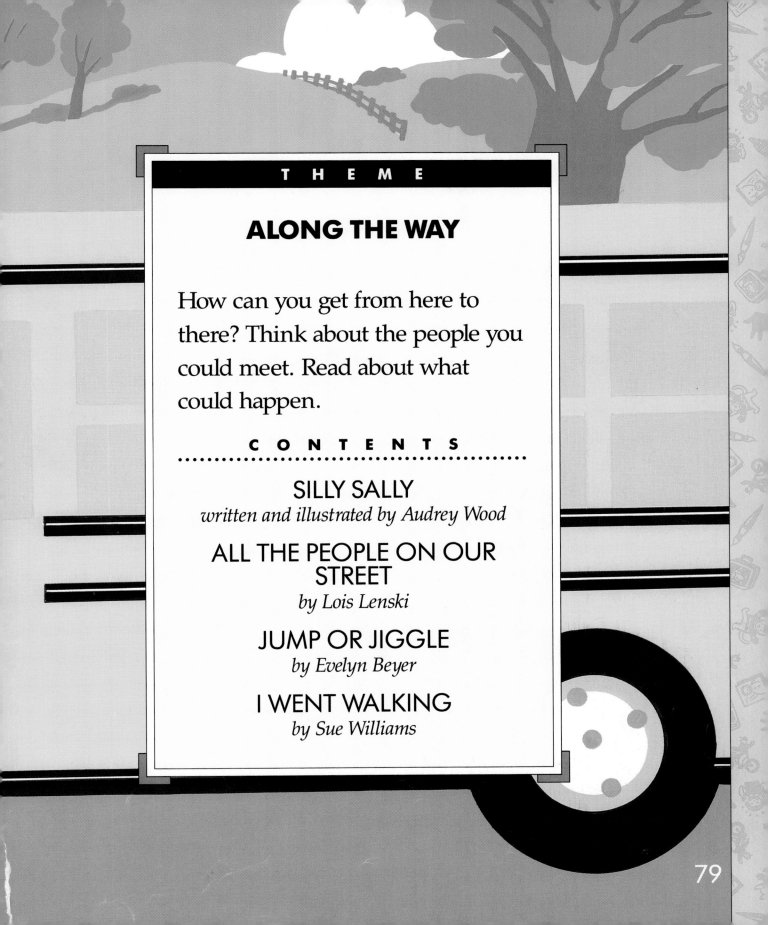

THEME

ALONG THE WAY

How can you get from here to there? Think about the people you could meet. Read about what could happen.

CONTENTS

Silly Sally

by Audrey Wood

Silly Sally went to town,
walking backwards, upside down.

On the way she met a pig,
a silly pig,

they danced a jig.

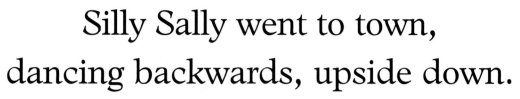

Silly Sally went to town,
dancing backwards, upside down.

87

On the way she met a dog,
a silly dog,

they played leap-frog.

Silly Sally went to town,
leaping backwards, upside down.

On the way she met a loon,
a silly loon,

they sang a tune.

Silly Sally went to town,
singing backwards, upside down.

On the way she met a sheep,
a silly sheep,

they fell asleep.

Now how did Sally get to town,
sleeping backwards, upside down?

Along came Neddy Buttercup,
walking forwards, right side up.

He tickled the pig
who danced a jig.

He tickled the dog
who played leap-frog.

He tickled the loon
who sang a tune.

He tickled the sheep
who fell asleep.

He tickled Sally
who woke right up.

She tickled Neddy Buttercup.

And that's how Sally got to town,

walking backwards, upside down.

All the People on Our Street

All the people on our street
Are people that I like to meet.
I like to walk and say hello
To all the people that I know.

by Lois Lenski

illustrated by Chris Lewis

AWARD-WINNING
AUTHOR

JUMP OR JIGGLE

written by Evelyn Beyer
illustrated by Julie Durrell

Frogs jump
Caterpillars hump

Worms wiggle
Bugs jiggle

Rabbits hop
Horses clop

Snakes slide
Sea gulls glide

Mice creep
Deer leap

Puppies bounce
Kittens pounce

Lions stalk—
But—
I walk!

I Went

Walking

AWARD-WINNING ILLUSTRATOR

I Went Walking

WRITTEN BY
Sue Williams

ILLUSTRATED BY
Julie Vivas

I went walking.

What did you see?

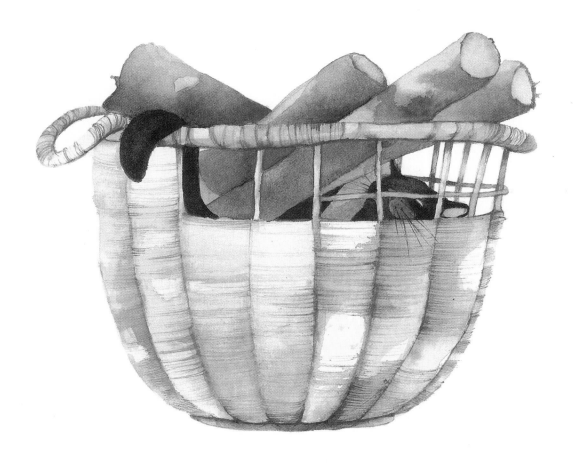

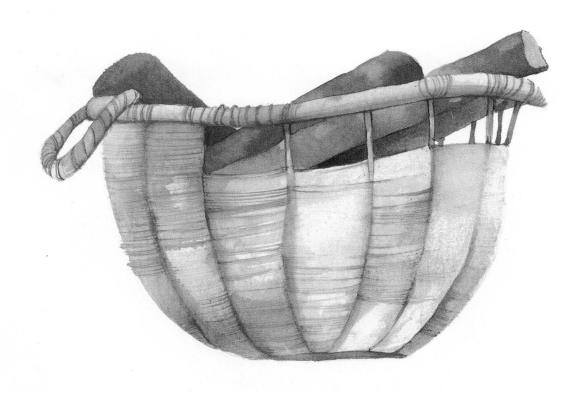

I saw a black cat
Looking at me.

I went walking.

What did you see?

I saw a brown horse
Looking at me.

I went walking.

What did you see?

I saw a red cow
Looking at me.

I went walking.

What did you see?

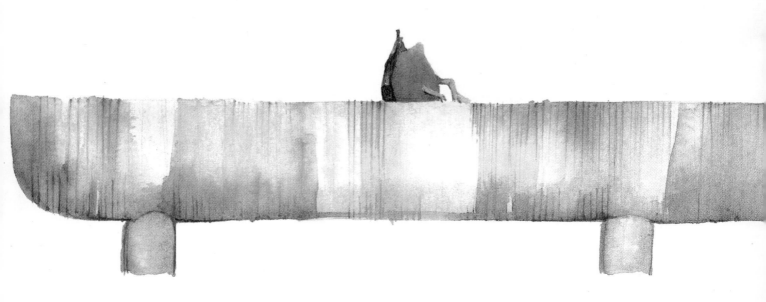

I saw a green duck
Looking at me.

I went walking.

What did you see?

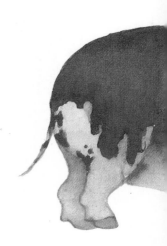

I saw a pink pig
Looking at me.

I went walking.

What did you see?

I saw a yellow dog
Looking at me.

I went walking.

What did you see?

I saw a lot of animals
Following me!